HOOD-MINTED

How Hustle, Faith and Fifty Cents Built an Empire

James [Monte] Montague

Disclaimer

Bible quotations identified within this book are taken from the New International Version.

Dedication

This book is dedicated to all the people in my life who have played a part in making me who I am today.

To my mother, Helen Montague—who raised me, supported me, and loved me throughout my life. If it weren't for her, I wouldn't even be here. Her love for the community has inspired me to step up my game and serve to the best of my ability.

To my beautiful wife, Wonza—my backbone and best friend.

To all of my family and friends—too many to name—much love to you all.

And finally, to my community of Southeast Raleigh, which is my heart and soul—much love to you all.

Peace and blessings. Enjoy!

Table of Contents

Introduction

Blessed are the hands that open the pages of this book, the eyes that read the words that I have written, and the ears that hear the words of my mouth. I have prayed and deeply meditated before asking God (Our Universal Creator) to open the windows of heaven and, again, pour us out blessings in the form of vibratory energy that will sweep over us like a giant wave of love. I asked to be used as a vessel for this act's purpose. Now that I've got that out of the way, thank you for taking a few minutes to show interest in my ideas, thoughts, and suggestions. I fully intend to make your life more prosperous and joyful through these few short chapters by sharing the *secret ingredients* I've used to become a highly successful real estate developer and owner of several multimillion-dollar businesses and properties.

Millionaire Pie

When I was a young boy, about seven years old, my Aunt Rachel would make my favorite Sunday dinner dessert— "Millionaire Pie!" It was so good! It had just the right amount of all the best ingredients. That pie was a family favorite and a requirement at all family events. I would watch her add each ingredient with love and patience, step by meticulous step, until each pie was done—only to be demolished by a line of family and friends eagerly waiting for it to be ready and cut. As I reflect on that process, I realize now that I learned many valuable lessons from both my mother and Aunt Rachel. I still use those lessons today as a foundation of my life and business.

Ingredients for Success

Separate and apart from each other, there's nothing special about the ingredients. Every single item used to make this pie can be picked up at the average grocery store. But when these ingredients are combined in carefully crafted measures, you've created something extraordinary. It becomes a masterpiece!

In the same way, when the average man or woman decides to do something magnificent with their life and begins doing ordinary things in an extraordinary way, success becomes almost certain. Beyond just working harder, true success also requires making the necessary changes to your mindset and personality. Like the pie, all the ingredients of success must be combined in the right proportions.

The first five ingredients for prosperity

To get this, you must first open your mind and be receptive to a new way of seeing a commonly used—but rarely understood—word: *"Information."* Let me break it down.

1.   The first thing you must recognize is the importance of fully buying into the concept of putting your brain to work differently. We must be committed—ready to go all in on becoming a new version of ourselves by changing how we see the world and how we see ourselves. Without taking this first step with boldness and dedication, transformation will be impossible, and continuing this journey would only be a waste of your time.

2.   Once you are open to receiving change, information from God and universal intelligence begins to move toward you—to do His work and fulfill His promises, which are guaranteed in the Word and in scripture.

Times may change, people may change, but the Word remains the same. It is His pleasure to inform us and guide us in His ways. This guidance can come through spoken words from our elders, reading books of wisdom, prayer, dreams, meditation, or even what seem like coincidences.

Meditation—meaning becoming familiar with yourself—is one of the most common ways we become informed.

3.   When God does His thing—which is to communicate a message—He does it by supplying details, giving instructions, and showing visions. This information is sent out on a wave of frequency, much like the incredible and powerful wave of radio.

The information is a blast of energy and insight that can only be received by those who are open and receptive to the signal. **Blessings!**

Those who are not tuned into the frequency won't be able to relate and may think those who *do* hear it are experiencing some sort of mental breakdown. But I can assure you, it's quite the opposite.

4.   Informed: At this stage, we have received the information, begun processing the thoughts, and started aligning with the Divine process. We have become aware of the presence of the Divine Mind. Like soldiers ready to carry out their mission upon receiving new marching orders, we are now willing. We are now **informed**.

5.   Information:

When the process of Divine dialogue begins, we gain a renewed sense of purpose. Our mission becomes clear. We begin to see the world as open and receptive to the will of God—which, when we are tuned to His frequency, becomes our will.

This means we are meant to carry a message through our actions, our attitude, and our work. When people witness the results of our efforts, they will not doubt that there is a power greater than man—one who works with and through us.

If this message feels familiar, it's because I learned it from Proverbs, chapter six, where God's Word instructs us to study the ways of the ant. I've done just that and have learned how ants operate, communicate, defend, build, and perform a host of other purposeful actions.

"...Which, having no guide, overseer, or ruler, provideth her meat in the summer, and gathereth her food in the harvest. How long wilt thou sleep, O sluggard? When wilt thou arise out of thy sleep?" (KJV)

In other words: When will we wake up to our potential?

I say the way is clear! Let's go. Wake up!

My entire business journey has been shaped by taking a deep look at the community that raised me. I found some of the best methods for solving the most common challenges in both my business and the greater community. I am deeply grateful to have been a positive force for change in my hometown.

Over the years, I've gained extensive experience in building and maintaining wealth by taking calculated chances and investing in real estate.

Building and maintaining wealth within underserved communities can be challenging—but it is absolutely achievable.

Here are 10 strategies I've learned.

1. **Start by empowering individuals with financial knowledge and skills.**
Offer workshops, seminars, and resources tailored to the specific needs and challenges of the community. We're set to open our first STEM center (Science, Technology, Engineering, and Math) this year in the newest shopping center—**Montague Plaza**. We'll implement this plan at that location. It's right beside a large high school and will be a valuable asset to the young people who attend and take advantage of our programs.

2. **Encourage and support entrepreneurship and small business development through local initiatives.**
Most cities and counties have grant money available to support these efforts, especially in underserved communities like the one where I grew up. These areas are common across both large and small cities, and investing in them creates real impact.

3. **Educate community members about the benefits of real estate investment.**
Encourage homeownership and provide resources to help individuals navigate the process of buying, selling, and investing in real estate. In my case, developing properties from the ground up has proven quite lucrative—and it can be for others as well.

4.   Start investment clubs and networks.

Pooling resources to invest collectively in stocks, bonds, mutual funds, and other strong investment opportunities is a wise and empowering strategy.

5.   Seek Professional Financial Guidance

There's always a big need for financial planning and wealth management services. Oftentimes, people in underserved areas overlook the advice of specialists in these fields—and end up paying dearly for that mistake. I've made that mistake myself before. That's why it's important to seek guidance and include someone certified in your network who can offer support with budgeting, saving, investing, and retirement planning.

While you're at it, you might as well add someone who can help strategize around your insurance needs. I once read a book called *What Would the Rockefellers Do?*—it was incredibly enlightening on this subject.

6.   Advocate for Access to Capital

Establish an advocacy group to increase access to capital and microfinance. Taking this step will significantly boost opportunities for small businesses in the community to secure the funding needed to launch—and for existing businesses to grow and thrive.

This can be done as part of your mission to offer assistance in the form of low-interest loans, grants, and other supportive resources.

7.   Build Community-Owned Businesses and Cooperatives

Strive to create community-owned businesses and cooperatives. This approach helps generate—and retain—

wealth within the community, while also encouraging collective ownership and decision-making.

These efforts can range from opening grocery stores to combat food deserts, to launching housing developments that address the critical need for quality, affordable housing—like the kind I've built.

8.   Establish Job Training Programs

Invest in programs that encourage young people and equip them with the skills and qualifications needed to secure high-paying jobs and advance in their careers. When we invest in our youth, we're investing in the future of our communities.

9.   Advocate for Financial Inclusion

We must push for greater access to fair, ethical banking services in underserved areas. Many of the financial institutions that do exist are predatory lenders—offering high-interest, low-opportunity services because they face no competition. Residents often feel they have no choice but to accept these terms. This must stop! But it will only stop when we collectively demand better options.

10.   Support Community Investment and Economic Development Initiatives

There is a great need for initiatives that prioritize the needs and interests of the Black community. By supporting policies and programs that confront systemic barriers to wealth creation, we can promote true economic empowerment and create lasting change.

Chapter 1: And There I Stood

The First Cut and Three Lessons That Shaped My Hustle

Paralyzed—frozen by fear—I played back in my mind what the 16-year-old neighborhood bully had just said to me. It was 1983, and I had just turned 13. We were standing in my mother's kitchen in the Southgate apartment projects of Southeast Raleigh. My mother had recently bought me some clippers from Kmart during a blue light special for $9.99.

Back in the day, our largest retail store was called Kmart, and every now and then, they would put certain items on special sale. You could spot these items by a flashing blue strobe light placed in the aisle. Shoppers would be browsing the store when, suddenly, an announcement would come over the intercom: the blue light special was in effect. Folks would rush to the aisle where the blue light was flashing.

And now—back to the story!

The bully looked me in the eyes and said, "Monte, do you hear me, boy?"

I nodded nervously, giving a weak grin. He repeated himself, this time with more force: "I swear God, if you gap my head, Imma beat your ass!"

Let me pause here to translate for those unfamiliar with the fine art of ghetto Ebonics. When someone from the hood begins a sentence with "I swear to God," they mean business. In this case, he was warning me: if I messed up his haircut, I

8

was going to need serious medical attention. And he wasn't bluffing—he was a big dude. I'd seen him beat up several people, and it was not pretty.

My hands shook as I wrapped the faded towel around his neck, securing it with an old wooden clothespin I grabbed from the clothesline out back. I still remember how my mind raced: *How did I get into this situation? How can I get out of it? Should I take off running if things go bad?* Then I remembered—we were in an apartment. There was nowhere to run.

At this point, I was sweating hard. My palms were so sweaty I had to keep wiping them on my shorts. I even started wondering if my wet hands would cause me to get shocked and electrocuted—just one more thing to worry about.

Eventually, I calmed down enough to focus. I realized the only way to get out of this situation unharmed was to *not* mess up his haircut. I had to stay focused on the task at hand.

Fortunately, I finished the cut without incident and walked away with my whopping fee of 50 whole cents. Not much money for the service—and certainly not worth risking my health and safety—but everybody has to start somewhere. My start just happened to be right there in the projects of Southgate.

Starting from such humble beginnings taught me how to serve others and to stay grounded. It also gave me three lessons that I still live by to this day:

1. Not All Money Is Good Money

Sometimes the cost of making money simply isn't worth the real price you end up paying. We all know someone who chased the promise of fast cash and ended up losing their freedom—or worse. You've got to weigh the trade-offs.

2. Start Where You Are with What You Have

I've heard so many people say things like, "If I had this amount of money, then I'd start." But that's not how it works for most business owners. Usually, an entrepreneur starts with an idea—and through boldness, persistence, and tenacity, they hold onto that dream. With patience and faith, they bring their vision into reality.

Don't get me wrong—business does require money. And that money must be earned by adding value to the lives of the people you serve. But money isn't what keeps you in business. It's about keeping promises. The promises you make to your customers, to your community, and—most importantly—to yourself.

You've got to commit from the beginning: *I will not quit. I will keep serving, even when it gets tough.* I talk a lot about challenges in my writing, and that's because too many people start businesses with unrealistic expectations. They underestimate how difficult it really is to achieve long-lasting success.

3. Don't Be Your Own Bully

We get upset when others doubt us or tell us we don't deserve success. But the harshest voice we face is often our own. The outside noise can't compare to the damage done by negative self-talk. A limited mindset is the biggest obstacle anyone can face.

If you keep telling yourself you can't do something, and you internalize that thought with strong emotion, your mind will accept it as fact. It will go to work making sure that failure becomes your reality.

If you've convinced yourself that you can't, then what's the point in trying?

We must guard our minds. We must protect ourselves from the inner bully at all costs.

Chapter 2: Rain, Rein, Reign — The Process for Prosperity

Can You Stand the Rain? Turning Tests into Testimonies

In every life, some rain must fall. In other words, anything you desire to accomplish will always meet resistance at the beginning. The bigger the vision, the stronger the resistance.

In the late '80s, there was a hit R&B song by New Edition called *Can You Stand the Rain*. That "rain" symbolized hard times—dark times of trouble, doubt, and uncertainty. Many people give up during this stage of stress, anxiety, and life's tests. But rain, in this context, marks the first step toward realizing your purpose. It doesn't feel like that in the moment—but with wisdom, patience, and understanding, you'll recognize it as a divine signal: *you're headed in the right direction.*

Understanding that this is part of the process brings peace. Knowing this is only the *first step* in a three-part journey should assure you that you'll make it through, and that everything will unfold in divine order.

The universal wisdom of God has already equipped us to handle even the most stressful situations. Scientifically speaking, how we perceive a situation directly affects our response—mentally, physically, and spiritually. If we view a situation as a *problem*, it can drain and discourage us. But if we reframe it as a *challenge*—something to overcome—we're energized. Our resolve is strengthened, and we are renewed with the power to push through any obstacle.

That mental shift is everything. When challenges come, we must quickly change how we view them. These aren't curses—they're chances to build resilience, strengthen character, and turn our test into a testimony.

By choosing to be proactive instead of reactive, we *grab the reins* and take responsibility for our outcomes. Picture a skilled horseback rider controlling a powerful animal 100 times their strength—calmly, with confidence. That's what we do when we take control of our mindset and our actions.

This is **Stage Two** of the process: showing our *response-ability*—our ability to respond with strength and wisdom.

At this stage, we realize that while we can delegate tasks, we can't escape responsibility. We must take credit when things go well—and take accountability when they don't. Things won't always go according to plan. But my mindset is this: *I don't lose—either I win, or I learn.* Every "loss" is really a lesson. And trust me—in my profession, those lessons can be expensive.

The key is not to get paralyzed by the fear of failure. Don't let setbacks define you. Instead, put on your game face and persevere. Remember: it can't rain every day. Natural law demands balance. After rain comes sunshine.

We must develop a mental image of the person we are becoming—our highest version. Visualize your future self: What kind of car do you drive? What do your surroundings look like? How do your relationships feel? How does your success show up in the world? What does your health look like? Do you travel the world?

Picture it all—in vivid detail. See the colors. Hear the sounds. Smell the air. But most importantly: *feel it*. How would it feel to be that version of yourself? The feeling is the key. Make it as real as possible in your mind.

Why? Because the mind doesn't know the difference between a real experience and an imagined one. Every feeling you create triggers a chemical reaction—whether the event happened or not. That energy affects your mind, body, and spirit.

The good news? You can use this to your advantage. The bad news? Most people use it to their *detriment*. Worry and doubt trigger a negative charge in the body—creating anxiety and fear, the opposite of faith.

It's impossible to dwell on negativity and produce positive results.

On the other hand, *positive* thoughts create positive feelings. These feelings generate proteins in the body that signal: *Get ready—your new reality is on the way.* The body becomes a magnet for the things you've imagined.

Sounds unbelievable? I'm a living witness. This has happened for me, over and over again. I call it putting my *faith into action*.

This isn't just my opinion. These are facts. Truly successful people know and apply these principles. I won't spend too much more time on this subject, but it's easy to prove by simply looking at the *opposite*—the destructive effects of chronic worry and negative thinking.

Most people dwell on worst-case scenarios. They imagine the worst things happening. And again—the mind doesn't know the difference. It reacts as if the imagined event is real. The body responds with the fight-or-flight reflex.

Stress kicks in. Anxiety takes over. And it becomes a downward spiral—until something greater lifts the mind and spirit out of darkness.

That's why we must be vigilant. Guard your thoughts. Doubt and fear are like seeds—if allowed to root in the mind, they'll grow into weeds that choke out your growth.

You must be a diligent gardener. Keep negative thoughts out of your mental garden. Pluck them up quickly. Destroy them before they destroy your peace, your purpose, and your power.

The Reign Begins

As we begin to understand the stages of the operation and the implementation process of *rain*, *rein*, and *reign*, it becomes clear that what we've experienced is truly the manifestation of *faith in action*—or what I call **F7**.

Having faith without taking control of the mind and then putting your thoughts into action is an example of *faith without works*. As the saying goes, "Faith without works is dead." This third step in the process of power is **reign**.

Let me be clear about the word *reign* and why I've included it in this book. Most of the time, when the word *reign* is used, it refers to a king ruling over a kingdom. This case is no different—except for one key distinction: I have no desire to be a king or to rule a kingdom of my own.

My objective is to live in the **kingdom of the Almighty—** God, Creator, Universal, and Omniscient. When we align with this frequency of God, we help *His* kingdom reign *here on Earth as it is in Heaven.*

We lead by example and draw more people into the truth of the power of His word. What's important to understand is that the principles that I've applied to life and business weren't invented by me. They are lessons I adopted from the wisdom of the elders as expressed and documented in biblical text.

Most of my study has been from the **Book of Proverbs** and **Ecclesiastes** in the **King James Version** of the Bible. Even though I've read both books several times over the years, I still gain new nuggets of wisdom—some meant to bless me directly, and others meant to be shared to bless someone else.

One of the best parts of being a highly sought-after business and thought leader is that I often find myself tested on my knowledge of business principles by folks who don't know me or my story. Some assume I'm just lucky or that I was born with a silver spoon in my mouth. I can assure you—with 100% certainty—neither is true.

The life I live is the result of **obedience to the precepts and principles of God's word**. There's also a strong mix of *stickability*, determination, and persistence—even in the face of adversity.

And I also happen to have been born and raised in the greatest country in the world—a nation with rules, laws, and a strong government. No country is perfect, and yes, we have our issues. But I'm still grateful and blessed to be a citizen of the United States.

Many of us take this blessing for granted. But I've traveled the world, and I can tell you firsthand: we are very fortunate to be U.S. citizens. No shade to any other country, but millions of people risk their lives and use their life savings trying to get here. Some even lose their lives in the process.

Thankfully, that's not a worry I've had to face—and for that, I'm truly grateful. I firmly believe that **gratitude leads to abundance**, and if we don't appreciate the small things, we'll never be able to see the big picture!

The Big Picture

This phrase is often overused but, in my opinion, rarely understood.

Most of my early adult life was devoted to the barber and cosmetology industry. I started cutting hair in my mother's kitchen in the Southgate Projects of southeast Raleigh when I was 14 years old. I charged 50 cents per head, and to be honest, when I first started—I sucked at it. Eventually, I became a master barber and platform artist for ladies' styles, but it took many years to develop those skills. I became one of the best barbers/stylists in the city and was even featured in a *Hair* magazine piece.

When I first started cutting hair in the kitchen, the hardest part was getting the hairline shaped up perfectly. Either the left side was too high, or the right side was too low. Now let me tell you something serious—if you want to see a brother get irate, mess up his hairline. So I had to learn to cut better— quickly, fast, and in a hurry.

One thing I learned to do at this early stage of my life—which I still do today in business—is to take a few steps back and look at the hairline from a distance. I'd check it out from a different angle and perspective. Once I learned to take my time and see how the whole haircut came together, I got much better. My lineups became perfect. I got so good I could cut all types of designs into hair. I even won design competitions at hair shows.

Enough about hair!

I use this principle of taking a step back in business by sometimes pausing and reflecting before making decisions in my real estate development work. I ask myself: What are the pros and cons of this action I'm about to take? Am I taking an unnecessary risk? Is the risk worth the potential reward?

The wise saying, *"An ounce of prevention is worth a pound of cure,"* couldn't be more accurate.

In my early years of real estate development, I made the mistake of getting emotional about a property or project and throwing caution to the wind.

Don't do that.

I got burned multiple times like that. And as much as I'd like to blame someone else, it was my responsibility to perform due diligence before making a major move. In the long run, blaming others for my issues didn't help me grow. At this point in history, **we are the authors of our own stories**. I refuse to be an extra in my movie. At the very least, I should be the main character in my own script.

Strong people don't make excuses or pass the blame for problems they created.

It's both humbling and empowering to assess a situation and say to yourself, *"Wow, I really messed this up—either through neglect or poor choices. How can I fix this? And if it's too late to fix, what can I do differently next time?"*

The most important part of a challenging situation is learning the **lesson from the test**.

In Proverbs 26:11, it says:
"As a dog returneth to his vomit, so a fool returneth to his folly."
What that means is: only a fool keeps making the same mistake over and over again without learning the lesson. Repeating the same mistake isn't a mistake anymore—it becomes a choice.

It seems crazy, but some people would rather make bad choices repeatedly than adjust their methods or processes. The truth is: change is scary. It requires venturing into unfamiliar territory. But to improve our skills and lives, we have to be willing to fall and get back up—drawing wisdom from the past without losing forward momentum.

The only way to have a better life and improve your reality is to **change your personality**. We must remain vigilant and **guard our minds against negative thoughts**, which, if acted upon, become detrimental actions. If not corrected, they solidify into habits. And over time, those habits shape our personalities.

On the opposite end of the spectrum are **positive and inspiring thoughts**. Positive thoughts align with a higher frequency and create a supercharged vibration. That energy seeks out others with similar vibrations, forming a wave of

pure power. Supreme Power seeks an outlet for expression in the physical realm.

It takes real effort to create long-term change. I've watched myself and others make changes, only to revert to old ways in just a few days. The issue is often that we're trying to change our actions without changing our internal identity. That's a **waste of time and energy**.

The greatest life-changing opportunities often show up disguised as impossible problems. But once we peel back the layers—like an onion (yes, there may be tears)—we find that the problem is really a chance to improve.

It's critical to understand that even when you're on the upswing and things are going well, **life is a cycle**. Eventually, the rain will come again. But this time, you'll have the wisdom and experience to handle it. You'll draw from your past lessons. That's how **wisdom is built**.

Each cycle may get harder, but God knows we are equipped to overcome. Your **test becomes your testimony**.

Confidence builds faith.
Faith builds hope.
Hope builds patience.
Patience builds persistence.
Persistence manifests into **works**.

And in the end, **we will all be remembered for the works that we manifest throughout our lives**.

Chapter 3: There is no Success without a Succession Plan!

Believe it or not, I am a novice gardener. The process of fruits and vegetation growing naturally is amazing. The idea that even the smallest seed, when planted in the proper environment and under the right conditions, can take root and eventually become a fruitful tree of its own is astonishing. Each seed contains within it the capability to duplicate itself and multiply abundantly. The seed even has enough intelligence to understand that its sole purpose for existing is to reproduce itself.

As beautiful and amazing as the journey is—from seed to full maturity—it is nothing in comparison to the limitless potential of man. For while a seed can only produce the fruit it came from, man, when aligned with his highest potential and a godly mindset, can create and become anything—or anyone—he chooses. That is true limitless potential.

Man can shape his success into whatever form he desires— whether as a successful businessman, a loving father, a superstar, an actor, a musician, or anything else. All he must do is bring up a clear and vivid mental image of himself living that life. Once the image is clear, he must fully feel what it would be like to live that reality.

Use your imagination to picture it down to the smallest detail. How would it feel if this life were already happening? What would it sound like? What sounds would you hear? What would you see? What would it smell like?

It is a scientific fact that the mind, when reaching this vivid state, cannot distinguish between imagined experience and lived reality. By making the image as real as possible, you begin creating your new reality!

The Plan for Secession

Too often—especially in communities of color—we see prominent or wealthy business leaders, often from various fields, who have worked hard their entire careers to provide for their families. Their goal has always been to ensure that the next generation could live a better life than their ancestors did. We have struggled and sacrificed for years in hopes that one day the future generation wouldn't have to work as hard to sustain and grow the business and its legacy.

The problem with this well-meaning approach is that most of the time, the next generation does not understand the foundational principles of the inherited business. Because they were not there at the beginning to witness the sacrifices, grit, and bold determination it took to start and grow the business from the ground up, they often take all that hard work for granted.

However, the fault doesn't solely lie with the heirs. The real shortcoming is often with the founder, who may not have put an implementable, long-term sustainability plan into the original business model from the very beginning.

Nothing should be left to chance when it comes to building a legacy. The more detail and structure you put into your succession plan, the better the chances the business will survive long enough to be considered a true multigenerational legacy business. In my opinion, any business that only lasts for one generation should not be considered a successful business.

The plan must also include enough flexibility to remain sustainable and agile—able to pivot when necessary in response to market changes such as war, regulatory shifts, economic disruptions, and unforeseen challenges. Over more than three decades in business, I've seen the market expand and contract multiple times.

My First Deal

For me, the journey into commercial real estate began at 918 Rock Quarry Rd., Raleigh, North Carolina. This project is called Statueside Business Plaza. It's a roughly 20,000-square-foot building located just blocks from downtown Raleigh in a rapidly gentrifying area.

Now, when I mention gentrification, there are really two sides to the word. For newcomers and transplants who have decided to move into a historically disadvantaged and divested community—one with a large Black population—the word means that the area is growing and has become a prime location for investment.

But for the people who were born and raised in this neighborhood, many of whom have lived here for generations, the term means something entirely different. Gentrification is viewed in an extremely negative light.

The word is almost like a curse. But I'll elaborate on this subject briefly.

The Statueside Business Plaza is leased to multiple tenants who have been there for decades. There are a variety of businesses ranging from childcare centers to beauty salons, tattoo shops, barbershops, event centers, real estate companies, and law offices.

I built that property after God blessed me with a dream—complete with all the details of the location, structure, and the activity that would take place on the site. The dream was delivered to me on a divine frequency in a sleep state in 1997, and the building was completed in 1998. So, we just celebrated the 25th anniversary of this real estate development.

From the beginning of this project, I was—and still am—very intentional about my tenant selection. I only lease space to small businesses that add value to the community and support our local area.

In other words, I'm not just trying to do anything to make a buck. Over the years, I have been approached by several prospective tenants who offered large sums of money to lease my buildings, but accepting those deals would most certainly have changed the character of the area—and not for the better.

I've also received multiple offers from people interested in purchasing the property outright. I've had no interest in selling.

The buyer would undoubtedly close the deal and then evict every business on the property. The impact on certain tenants, their families, and the broader community would be devastating. Our mission at F7 is never to create a dilemma with that kind of outcome—but unfortunately, this very scenario is happening all over our city and in many other cities and states around the country.

The Reality of Gentrification: A Southside Reflection

Take a walk with me through the Southside experience. Imagine you were born and raised in an area where your parents, grandparents, and probably their parents before them were born. Then one day, you wake up and realize all your familiar neighborhoods are gone. The people you've known and been friends with your entire life have been replaced by total strangers. Not only are these new neighbors unfamiliar, but suddenly, *you* and your family are the outcasts—strangers in your own community.

To make matters worse, you open your mailbox and discover that your property taxes have skyrocketed—40% to 50% higher than they were the previous year. You're bombarded by an endless stream of callers trying to convince you that your property is worthless and that you should be grateful they're gracious enough to "take it off your hands." The goal? To banish you and your family to the outskirts of your own city, where once again, you're unwelcome.

This time, you have no connections, no political power, no equity—and most importantly, no understanding of who's really making the decisions that will shape the future of your life and your family's life. The worst part? Because of the inflated value of homes in your own community, the place you've called home your whole life is now financially out of reach. You may never return as a resident.

Maybe you think this didn't happen by chance—and you'd be right. It was planned. Years ago. By city leaders who never truly considered your people. You were seen not as residents but as obstacles to "progress." In many places, **urban renewal** has essentially meant **Black removal**.

But let me be clear—**all hope is not lost**.

Over my 35 years in business, one of the most important lessons I've learned is this: the greatest opportunities are often disguised as seemingly impossible situations. The rarest and most valuable elements on earth are always buried under the most dirt and subjected to the most pressure.

Sometimes, that pressure comes from our own past mistakes or neglect. But other times, it comes because it's time to rise— to be elevated to the next level in life or business.

The key is to resist the urge to rush the process or make emotional decisions that could cost you dearly in the long run. Every situation deserves careful thought. And often, the best move is to seek guidance from elders or experienced professionals in the industry you're navigating. Their wisdom can help you avoid costly mistakes and save you time and energy that could be better used elsewhere.

As a more seasoned gentleman, I often reach out to younger folks through email or phone, trying to offer some direction. You'd be surprised how many successful people are willing to mentor or advise if approached the right way. Just don't waste their time.

Be respectful. Be mindful. Understand—they don't *owe* you anything. If you reach out, skip the small talk and get to the point. Ask your question. Listen carefully to the feedback. And most importantly, follow through. You don't have to implement everything they say, but if someone takes the time to speak positivity into your life and then finds out you took no action—it's unlikely they'll invest in you again.

That time will be seen as a waste—time that could've been given to someone who at least tried to grow something from the seed.

After all, you can't plant a seed in a shoebox with no light or water and expect it to bear fruit.

Check Yourself Like You'd Check Anybody Else

Picture this. You're having a great day. The sun is shining, the birds are chirping, and there's a fresh spring breeze in the air. You're walking down the street and spot a group of people you consider friends or associates. You walk over to greet them with positive energy and open gestures.

But as you get closer, you realize they're deep in a serious conversation. And then it hits you—the conversation is about you. Not only that, they're dragging your name through the mud, talking negatively about your character, your abilities, and your supposed failure to get things done.

You step into the group, and they see you—but instead of stopping, they double down. They say it all to your face: "You're no good." "You should give up." "You can't do it."

Now pause right there. In that moment, how would you respond? If you're the polite type, maybe you'd calmly let them know they're wrong and that they shouldn't speak about you that way. But let's be real—if you're not so nice, you might cuss them out and make a scene. Either way, you're going to **check them**, right? You're going to make it known that you will not tolerate that kind of disrespect. And rightfully so.

So here's the question:

Why don't you check yourself that way when your own inner voice starts doing the same thing?

Why is it that when those negative thoughts and voices come from within—when *you* start questioning your own abilities, doubting your value, tearing yourself down—you just let it happen? You let those words bounce around in your head unchecked. And when that happens long enough, those thoughts get absorbed by your **subconscious mind**, which immediately goes to work trying to fulfill what it believes is your desire. It turns those thoughts into a plan—and before you know it, they're showing up in your real life.

That's why you've got to learn to **shut it down**, just like you would if it came from someone else. When negative self-talk creeps in, correct it fast. Get yourself straight and do it with the same urgency you'd use to check a hater on the street.

Here's the truth:
The things other people say about you don't matter nearly as much as what **you** say about yourself.
Your **mind is fertile soil**. And like any garden, it can grow flowers or weeds—it all depends on what you plant. Whatever you nurture will take root and multiply.

So it's in your best interest to **silence that inner critic** and plant seeds of belief, hope, and positivity. Replace destructive thoughts with strong, empowering ones. Imagine your success. Feel the energy of your goals already achieved. The more vivid the vision, the more deeply it's impressed into your subconscious. And just like that, the cosmic forces align to bring it to life.

Get yourself straight—and keep yourself straight!

Chapter 4: Never Underestimate the Positive Power of Pain

It's no secret that in every life, there comes some sort of pain now and then. Of course, some people seem to experience more pain than others, but no one is immune to difficulties and heartaches that, in the moment, feel like they'll last forever.

Throughout my business and personal life, I've experienced some very tough challenges that brought extremely high levels of stress and pressure. At times, I wondered if I'd make it through with my mind intact. One vivid example of this kind of painful memory happened during the 2008 recession, when I got a call from the bank that held the note on one of my largest shopping centers in Greensboro, North Carolina: the *Dudley Lee Cultural Commercial Center* at 709 E. Market St.

I bought that property in 2003 for $3.2 million. At the time, it felt like a great deal because it was valued at over $4.1 million—meaning I had about $1 million in equity from the start. When I acquired the center, it was only about 30% leased, with 70% of the space sitting vacant. I lived about an hour away and wasn't familiar with the area, so it took a few years to build relationships with the local community and get those spaces filled.

But I got it done. Everything seemed to be going great—until one day in June 2008, when I received a phone call that rocked my world and sent me into a spiral that took years to recover from. Here's how the call went:

Banker: Hello, James. Do you have a minute to speak?

Me: Sure, what's up?

Banker: Listen, I've got some bad news and some... sort of good news.

Me: OK, give me the bad news first.

Banker: We're going to need to be paid out.

Me: OK... I just made a payment last week.

Banker: No, Monte. We need the full remaining balance of your loan—$2.8 million.

Me: What?! Why?

Banker: Our board reviewed the portfolio, and with the impending recession, we're working to reduce exposure. We need to eliminate some of our larger debts to strengthen the bank's balance sheet.

Me: OK... and what's the so-called *good* news?

Banker: You have 30 days to pay us out.

Me: Well, damn, sir! That ain't good news. You should've just lumped that in with the bad! Thirty days isn't enough time to come up with $2.8 million—especially when it blindsides you like that!

The next 30 days were some of the most stressful, painful days of my life. The feeling of loss and hopelessness took me totally out of my element. I was angry. I blamed the bank. I blamed the economy. I blamed everyone—except the person who was most responsible: **me.**

How could I not have seen this coming?

Why wasn't I prepared for the ups and downs of the lending environment?

Why didn't I have a network of partners who could help me fight this battle?

At the time, I was too ashamed to ask for help. I didn't want to show any signs of weakness in business, so I kept it all to myself. When the 30 days were up, I had no choice but to sign the property over through a *Deed in Lieu of Foreclosure*—and just like that, I walked away from $1.8 million in equity. Equity that took me years to build.

I could sit here and tell you it didn't hurt. I could act like it didn't break me. But I'd be lying.

After I left that bank in 2008, I cried like a baby in the car. I had to pull over on the side of the road, and I remember beating the steering wheel, trying to release all that pain. When the tears dried, I pulled myself together and asked:

What did I learn from this?

What would I do differently?

How can I protect my business from this kind of pain in the future?

The worst part? The bank ended up selling the shopping center for far less than what I owed. Then they came after me for the $1 million difference I had personally guaranteed. That was the double whammy—a judgment that nearly put me out of business. And once you have a judgment like that on your record as a small business owner, it's damn near impossible to buy, finance, or refinance anything until it's paid off.

When I finally met with an attorney, he advised me to file for bankruptcy. But I couldn't do it.

I made a decision: I would fight this thing with everything in me. And that's exactly what I did.

I paid off the judgment over the next three years and came back stronger than ever. With renewed confidence. With renewed purpose. With a fire in me that still burns to this day.

And here's what I learned through it all:

Pain + Reflection = Progress

It's a waste of life and energy to go through hardship and never take time to reflect. You've got to find the wisdom in the wreckage. If you go through hell and don't walk out with something that strengthens your mind, body, or spirit, you haven't grown—you've just been *damaged*.
And that, my friend, is what I would call a self-imposed torment.

Chapter 5: Cut the Tangled Parachute Quickly

We've all seen it in the movies—a skydiver jumps out of a plane at a high altitude, and if they're smart, they've packed a backup parachute along with the main one.

Sometimes, while descending, something goes wrong. The main parachute doesn't open properly—maybe there's a failure with the cord, or it gets tangled and doesn't fully deploy. Now it's a serious situation. Life or death. A smart, prepared jumper has a backup chute for exactly this reason.

But here's the thing: if the faulty chute is still flapping uselessly overhead, the jumper is still in danger. If they engage the backup chute while the bad one is still attached, it can get tangled in the mess—and they're doomed. That's why an experienced jumper carries a sharp knife. In a moment of urgency, they pull it out and **cut loose the defective chute**, giving the backup enough space to open cleanly—and saving their life.

The reason I'm using this example is because **it's a perfect metaphor for the danger of holding onto bad habits**. Like that tangled parachute, bad habits can weigh you down and put your life, purpose, and potential at risk.

There's a common misconception that you can play around with bad behavior and still expect good results. But the truth is: **over time, your habits become your personality—**

and if you don't deal with them swiftly, they can take over your identity.

Once you've identified a harmful pattern, it's not enough to "tinker" or "ease out" of it. You must **cut the cord completely**—just like the skydiver does in a crisis. Otherwise, your new life—your backup chute—won't be able to open.

To truly break free, you have to **become a different person**.

Here's a real-life example:
Let's say someone is a heavy drinker and decides to stop for medical reasons or to improve their quality of life. The common mistake is saying, "I'm *trying* to stop drinking."

What does that imply?
That they still identify as a drinker.

Instead, they should say, **"I'm not a drinker."**
That's a powerful, decisive identity shift.

It means you're no longer someone who is *interested* in drinking. You're not someone who's merely resisting temptation—you've moved on. You've become someone new.

That's the first step in transforming your habits and your life:
Cut the tangled chute cord so your new self can rise.
There's no room for faulty habits in your future. Let them go—for good.

Chapter 6: Playing with My Money Is Like Playing with My Emotions

One of the funniest movies of all time is *Friday*, starring rapper Ice Cube and comedian Chris Tucker. It was the perfect mix of hood, comedy, and action that kept your attention.

There's one unforgettable scene where the local drug plug, Big Worm—played by Faizon Love—is talking to Smokey, an amateur drug seller and full-time pothead played by Chris Tucker.

Smokey had been smoking more of Big Worm's weed than he was selling, and as a result, the money he owed was coming up short. Big Worm, visibly fed up, looked at Smokey and said, **"Playing with my money is like playing with my emotions."**

When I heard that line, it hit me differently. I started thinking—**what if I could somehow leverage my internal emotions to become a magnet and attract wealth** just by adjusting my mindset?

If it's true that we become what we think about, then thinking thoughts of **lack, fear, and failure** will only bring those experiences to us. But when we **adjust the polarity of that mental magnet**—shifting toward thoughts of **wealth, health, prosperity, and wholeness**—we begin to attract those things instead.

By using and maintaining a **positive mental attitude**, we create space for positive results to show up. And the key to making this happen is to **internalize the emotions** of already having what we desire. When you *feel it*, your subconscious mind doesn't know the difference between imagined success and real success.

It's natural for weak, negative thoughts—fears, doubts, panic—to creep in. They always will. That's part of being human. But when they do, **you must guard your mind** like it's a fortress and fight hard to keep those thoughts from breaching the gates.

It's a never-ending battle. Get used to it. Better yet—**get good at it.**

Most people think that successful folks don't have thoughts of doubt or lack. That's not true. In fact, we often have **more** of those thoughts than the average person—we just refuse to let them stay. We're committed to deleting, blocking, and replacing them.

We take the reins of our future into our own hands. We don't wait around for luck—we **pick up the hammer and chisel** and start carving away at the slab of our lives.

Only instead of chipping away at marble, we chip away at **negative thoughts** and **bad habits**, until we uncover the version of ourselves that we want to become.

We transform our lives by changing our reality. And we change our reality by transforming our personality.

Chapter 7: Building your Skill

In January 2001, I became an **unlimited licensed general contractor** in North Carolina. This certification was a *huge* deal for me at the time. I was one of the youngest Black unlimited licensed general contractors to hold that classification in the entire state—and the youngest in my hometown of Raleigh, North Carolina.

I took great pride in finally being licensed and thought that from that point forward, I'd be cruising down Easy Street.

Boy, was I wrong.

I assumed I'd instantly be able to compete with the bigger companies for state and government contracts. For years, I tried. But what I didn't realize was that those companies had **decades of relationships, insider connections, and experience**—and they knew how to play the game at a much higher level than I ever knew existed.

It was a **humbling experience**, and it forced me to step back and reassess. I had to take a hard look at my strengths and weaknesses. While doing that exercise, I gained clarity on what my **niches** would be.

I decided to start **building my own small-scale projects** from the ground up. Then I'd keep and manage my assets to grow my portfolio. I started with shopping centers, then moved on to apartments and single-family homes. Today, I've expanded into **mixed-use development** in multiple cities— and I still have several projects in the pipeline.

None of these projects have been easy. But no one ever said that real estate development was supposed to be.

I've stumbled every step of the way. And each time I fall, I **dust myself off, get back up**, and reflect on the lesson embedded in the experience. Every lesson becomes part of my **mental playbook**—and when the time is right, I pull that play and execute with intention.

At this stage of my career, I've become highly efficient in real estate development. I am—and always will be—a **student of the game**. I'm constantly studying new methods and evaluating how I, and my company **F7 International Development**, can grow to the next level.

The Changing Face of Development

When I first started in real estate development back in 1997, land and property values in Southeast Raleigh were **relatively cheap**. At the time, I could buy an acre of land for about **$15,000–$20,000**. I bought my first new house in that same community for just **$67,000**—a three-bedroom, two-bathroom home on one-third of an acre near good schools and in a solid neighborhood.

Fast forward to today. That same area now has **.12-acre lots** going for around **$275,000**, which means over **$1 million per acre**. The house I once bought for what seemed like pennies on the dollar would now be valued at **$500,000 at minimum**, and even that would be considered a rare find. Many of the homes being built in the area now exceed **$1 million** in value. I just finished building a house at **516 New Bern Avenue**, and the tax value alone is over **$1.2 million**, and it's not even 3,000 square feet.

Costs are continuing to rise with no signs of slowing down. Based on recent sales history, there's no indication that property values will drop anytime soon. As you can imagine, this new reality has led to rampant **gentrification and displacement**—a process that feels all too intentional. In fact, it seems like this was the city's **long-term plan** all along. Oh wait... **it was**.

Assets vs. Liabilities

With all the distractions we face daily, it's easy to lose focus. But the way to prosper, grow, and maintain a sustainable lifestyle is simple: **always keep your liabilities lower than your assets**.

It doesn't matter whether you're an employee or an entrepreneur—you must never lose sight of this principle.

There's a small passage in the Bible that backs this up. In **Proverbs 11:26**, it states:

"He that withholdeth corn, the people shall curse him: but blessing shall be upon the head of him that selleth it."

Hold up—before you get confused, let me explain. This passage isn't just talking about *literal* corn. The "corn" here is symbolic. It represents the **personal value** each of us brings to the market in exchange for money.

For some, it's time.
For others, it's wisdom.
For most, it's goods and services.

The amount of goods or services you sell, minus what it costs to produce them, is your **profit**. This is why understanding the difference between **assets** and **liabilities** is key.

Many people get this twisted. They think their **house or car is an asset**, but unless you're making money off those things, they are actually **liabilities**. A **personal-use car** is a liability. The same goes for your **residence** if it's not generating income.

Examples of **real assets**:

- Rental homes
- Apartment complexes
- Shopping centers
- Books for sale (like this one), that provide long-term income and share knowledge

Even **your body and mind can be assets** in this era of evolving technology.

If you're **6'10"** with a **48-inch vertical**, there's a strong chance you can monetize that physical gift. Agents and scouts would be eager to help you cash in—because **they benefit, too**.

Or, if you're a **smart, driven young woman** with natural charisma and ambition, you can leverage your **talents and presence** to build a brand and succeed in nearly any industry you pursue. Social media and digital platforms like **YouTube, TikTok, and Instagram** have opened the door for **everyday people to engage wide audiences** and generate wealth by turning their gifts into value.

That said—**beware of scams**. The internet is also filled with **false promises** of instant success, designed to prey on people's dreams and **rob them of their hard-earned money**.

The Bottom Line: Net Worth

The best assets are the ones that generate income **constantly and consistently**.

Assets – Liabilities = Net Worth

That's the real scorecard of life.

Can someone be considered truly successful **without a healthy balance sheet**? Not likely. Your **net worth** is a reflection of how well you manage your resources, time, and value.

Any serious business should have a solid **team**—and that team should absolutely include a **good Accountant**. Your finances are the foundation of your future. Build them wisely.

The Mastery Mindset: 10,000 Hours and the Power of Persistence

It is a widely accepted belief that to become a **master of a skill**, it takes roughly **10,000 hours** of focused, dedicated effort. I've witnessed this truth play out time and time again. Because of my own experiences and observations, it would be hard to convince me otherwise.

But let's be clear—those hours can't be filled with **halfhearted effort**. Mastery requires **commitment**, **discipline**, and a willingness to constantly improve by trying new approaches. You will **fail**, just like we all do. But then you **learn**, adjust, and try again.

This cycle—**try, fail, learn, repeat**—must happen repeatedly. With each iteration, you improve, inch by inch. Eventually, you start to understand that even the failures are

an essential part of the process. You only truly fail when you **give up and stop trying**. That's when defeat wins.

Now, I'm not saying it's easy to fall short over and over again. It's tough. But that's where **faith** comes in. Your belief in what's possible has to rise up and push you forward toward your **goals, dreams, and vision** of success. With time and repetition, your efforts begin to feel **second nature**. You develop **muscle memory**. You move from conscious effort to effortless action. And that's when you know—**you're mastering your craft**.

But the most important thing to remember on this journey? **Never believe you've learned everything there is to know** about a subject or skill. The moment you start thinking that, you stop growing. There's always room to improve. There's always more to learn

.

Chapter 8: Mirror, Mirror

There is nothing more humbling than leaving an important meeting, looking into a mirror, and realizing your shirt is buttoned wrong, your tie is crooked or stained, something green is stuck between your teeth—or worst of all—there's been something hanging out of your nose all day.

Maybe you woke up late or got dressed in the dark. Whatever the case, all of those embarrassing outcomes could have been easily avoided by simply checking the mirror while getting dressed.

This same kind of **self-reflection** is necessary in business and in life. Every now and then, we need to evaluate our procedures and processes to make sure our systems are running efficiently. We must ensure that our **mission still aligns with our mission statement**, and that our company's **core values don't erode over time**.

Even in our personal lives, reflection is crucial. Are we treating the people around us the way we'd want to be treated? Are we being fair? I believe in **karma**—what we do to others comes back to us multiplied. That's why it's so important to examine our **behavior patterns** regularly. If unchecked, negative patterns can become bad habits, and those habits can form damaging long-term personality traits that lead to self-destruction.

By now, you understand: a mirror is deeper than something you simply use to admire your physical appearance.

Scripture emphasizes this point in **James 1:23–25**, where it says that a person who hears the word but doesn't live by it is like someone who looks in a mirror, sees their reflection, and immediately forgets what they looked like. But the person who looks into the **perfect law of liberty**—God's divine principles—and actually applies them is the one who will be blessed in their actions.

The **first mirror** is the kind we all know—the literal reflection of ourselves. The **second mirror** is the one we don't often talk about: the human ability to **observe, study, and mimic** the behaviors of others we admire. Whether we're aware of it or not, we naturally **mirror** the people around us.

In underserved communities like the one I grew up in, too many young people mirror the wrong examples—often those heading down destructive paths. My hope is that this book offers **alternative examples** to mirror—examples that reflect **smart, disciplined choices** and lead to **wealth, peace, and purpose**.

You don't need to copy every detail of someone else's journey. But you can **borrow the habits that align with your values**, and leave behind what doesn't serve you. That's the beauty of the internet today—you can learn lessons from people all over the world and throughout history. I've studied individuals from all walks of life, and not everything I've learned worked for me. Some methods were too harsh or didn't align with my beliefs. But others—those that **resonated with my spirit**—I've successfully incorporated into my life and business.

Not every idea you try will succeed. Some things are harder than they appear from the outside looking in. But that's the value of **trial and error**. I still believe it's worth the effort.

My objective is to become an **example of success that young people can relate to**. I want to plant a **seed of possibility** in the subconscious mind—so that when the conditions are right, that seed can **sprout and grow**, producing good fruit and more seeds for the next generation.

Here's the challenge: we've got to **resist the urge to rush the process**.

It sounds silly, but it's like planting a seed in good soil, then digging it up the next day to see if it's grown. That's what many of us do with our lives—we make a good decision, expect instant results, and when we don't see them, we give up.

Take dieting, for example. Someone eats poorly their whole life, then decides to eat healthy for a week and steps on the scale expecting to see 10 pounds gone. **That's not how life works**.

Instant results rarely last. True results take **time, patience, and sacrifice**.

People look at others who've succeeded and assume it all came overnight. What they don't see are the **sleepless nights, the stress, the discipline, the sacrifices**—the full price paid for success. No matter what the ads and social media posts promise, there is no shortcut. And the mirror will always tell the truth.

Chapter 9: Tests are not Supposed to be Easy

You will never hear anyone say, "This test was easy; I learned so much from it." In fact, the more difficult or challenging a situation is, the more you learn from it. People who have been through the toughest battles and truly understand the process of growth have the unique ability to convert their challenges into solutions that build character.

Success is not measured by the things you buy or how much money you have. True success is determined by who you become along the journey. People often say, "Success is not a destination, but a journey," and that couldn't be more accurate.

When I first reached a modest level of success, I'd get hyped up whenever I accomplished a big goal. But I quickly realized that the enthusiasm faded after hitting the mark. I'd soon find myself chasing the next goal to bring back that rush of emotion. I was hooked on the feeling—on the outside validation and recognition.

But over time, I learned that true joy had to come from within. I didn't need outside validation to be happy with myself. And **neither do you**.

What Life's Tests Reveal

Here are a few things that life's tests will reveal to you:

1.   Who are you?

2.   Why are you here?

3.   How strong are you?

4.   Do you really believe in yourself—and in God?

Managing Partner

I am the President and CEO of **F7 International Development**, a real estate and general contracting company I founded to serve my community. My vision has always been to spark economic development—first locally, then nationally, and eventually internationally.

Admittedly, I own several large commercial and residential buildings, as well as single-family homes. It's taken years of hard work and millions of dollars to build and acquire these assets.

By definition, a **managing partner** is the highest-ranking executive in a firm who oversees strategy, operations, finances, and culture. I won't argue with that—it's an accurate and widely accepted definition.

But for me, the role of **managing partner** means something deeper.

Yes, I may own these properties on paper. But I also understand the greater reality: as I write this, I'm 54 years old. The average lifespan in the U.S. is about 75. That means every day is precious—and every day, we inch closer to our expiration date.

But **the Word of God never expires**.

I've based my company's success not on luck or hustle alone, but on a relationship with **God, our Father**. That makes me not the true CEO—but a **managing partner of God's assets**.

I manage what He's entrusted to me while I'm here on this earthly journey. I'm not confused. I know that business often looks like a race to accumulate as many material things as possible. But I don't live there. I understand I can't take any of this with me, so why stress over it? **I'm here to enjoy life and serve well while I have the time.**

Stewardship, Not Ownership

I study daily to be a good steward of the blessings God has allowed me to obtain and use. I will not waste His time or resources. Each day, I work to improve in my assignments, knowing the true goal is to **bless as many people as possible** and **give honor where it's due**.

The **projects** I've built were manifested by God and given to me in spirit before they ever came into existence. I could easily take credit, but that would defeat the purpose. I've witnessed miracles—situations no one else could solve, where help didn't come from man, but from **Him**.

Too many times, I've been at the end of my rope, and just when I was about to give up, **God sent a sign**—a person, a moment, a breakthrough. Something to say, **"I got your back, son. You're not alone."**

Thrown Into the Deep End

This divine pattern has strengthened my faith and built up my confidence to take on challenges most would never consider. I've learned to take pleasure in the process because I know **the test strengthens the testimony**.

It reminds me of those videos of parents teaching infants to swim. They throw the baby into the water—and miraculously, the baby kicks, floats, and swims! It's as if they were born with the **blueprint** for survival already inside of them.

That's the kind of faith we need. I truly believe God won't let me drown. And if He does, it's for a reason—it was meant for a purpose. And I'm good with that.

I've faced so many situations that seemed hopeless, where I thought the end was near—then boom! A miracle. A breakthrough. A prayer answered. A way made clear.

The Easy Way Isn't Always the Right Way

The **easy way** may look like the best way, but it's rarely the **right way**. The struggle strengthens you. The pressure prepares you. And the pain produces wisdom.

In every chapter of my life—every business move, every personal trial—I've seen the **hand of God**. And I now know that my title, my success, and my strength all come from Him.

I'm just the managing partner.

Chapter 10: Take it Personal

On the morning of **March 24, 2024**, I fell into a deep meditation, followed by prayer, and I asked God to direct me in the way of His Will.

What I *expected* to receive on the frequency of thought was a pat on the back—for all the projects I had completed and the many real estate development initiatives F7 International Development has on the drawing board. But instead, what I got was a swift kick in the spiritual butt.

I was led to scriptures that focus on the *lazy man*. In fact, there were several scriptures—all of them centered on the **ant** and its ability to work prophetically and efficiently.

I tried for hours to wriggle free from the constructive criticism coming from on high. After all, who wants to admit to themselves that they're not doing all they can in life?

Any time you see ants, they're not just staying busy—they're *working with purpose*. They're searching for food for the colony, building the mound, developing real estate, protecting their homes, policing the neighborhoods, moving the larvae, and guarding the queen. You'll never catch an ant just *chilling* or being complacent.

As much as I hate to admit it, after many years of success in business, **I had become complacent**.

Reclaiming the Reins

My solution for feeling complacent was to **take the reins** and start doing things in a new way.

I've begun to share the knowledge I've gathered throughout my real estate and business career. At this stage of my life, I've forgotten more than most people even know about real estate. So here goes—**my best version of how to accomplish the mission.**

My No-Money-Down Techniques

When I first started acquiring real estate, I had to get creative—not just because I *wanted* to succeed, but because I didn't have a lot of credit, had **very limited cash**, and no proven track record to leverage like I do now.

Buying real estate with no money down can be challenging, but it's possible. These methods require creativity, negotiation skills, and a good understanding of real estate investment. Below are the five best ways I've personally used to buy real estate with no money down:

1. Seller Financing

Negotiate with the seller to finance the purchase instead of going through a bank. The seller becomes your lender. You agree on terms like interest rate and repayment period and make payments directly to them. This works especially well if the seller is motivated or flexible. Keep your proposal *plain and simple* to avoid confusion later.

2. Joint Ventures & Partnerships

Find partners or investors who are willing to fund the purchase. Offer them a share in the property or a return on their investment. This method requires building strong relationships. Just be cautious—once, I sent someone too much info without a **non-compete, non-circumvent**

agreement, and they went around me. Don't let that happen to you—get that agreement signed first!

3. Wholesaling
Find distressed properties at a low market value and **assign the contract** to another buyer for a fee. You're acting as the connector between motivated sellers and cash buyers. You may not buy the property yourself, but you still earn through the **assignment fee**.

4. Lease Option
Lease the property with the **option to buy** it later. Negotiate the purchase price and lease term upfront. While leasing, save up or work on getting financing to exercise your purchase option.

5. Creative Financing
This is one of my go-to strategies. Explore options like **private money lenders, hard money loans**, or use your network to find interested investors. Private loans often have fewer requirements than traditional banks. Hard money loans are short-term, high-interest loans usually secured by the property itself.

These methods help you **get your foot in the door** and seize opportunities in today's hot real estate market.

If one of these methods doesn't work on your first try, **don't give up**. Try again. Make small adjustments to your technique. **Be patient. Have faith. Persevere.**

Eventually, it *will* work.

Chapter 11: Be the Original

My career path started out humbly—cutting hair as a kid in my mom's kitchen in the projects during the early 1980s. From there, I learned a new skill in cosmetology in the 1990s, which I practiced for many years. Then, in the late 1990s, I was given a dream to pursue commercial development, and in 1998, I built my first shopping centers soon after.

In 2001, I bought my first 13-acre tract of land specifically for residential senior housing and developed **Elders Peak Retirement Community**, just two blocks from Southgate—the projects where I grew up.

My newest endeavor, launching soon, will focus on **information, technology, and investment**.

This journey has been a unique mix of highs and lows. The wins and losses have made me who I am today. But that's not why you bought this book.

You bought this book to learn how to leverage the hard lessons I've learned over the years to benefit your **business, personal life, and spiritual growth**—without having to go through all the pain. At least, that's why I would be reading it.

No one can be a better **you** than *you*. We can all improve the way we do most things by studying successful people and incorporating aspects of their approach into our own lives. Even when you adopt their methods, you're still being yourself.

With technology advancing so rapidly, there are now *countless* paths to success. Since I'm already talking about ways to prosper financially, here are a few **benefits of being original** in both life and business:

1. Being Original

This sets you apart from the crowd and gives you a **competitive advantage** in the global marketplace. It helps you create a unique selling proposition that attracts customers and differentiates your business. By offering something distinct and innovative, you can win the attention and loyalty of customers who crave fresh ideas and solutions—which, these days, is just about everybody.

2. Brand Identity

Establishing your business as original creates a **strong brand image** that resonates with your target audience. A unique brand builds trust and recognition, making it easier for customers to remember and choose your products or services over others.

3. Market Disruption

Originality often leads to **disruptive ideas and business models**. By challenging conventional norms, you introduce new concepts, incorporate technology, and add significant value to the market. Disruptive businesses have the power to shift entire industries, gain major market share, and leave a lasting legacy.

4. Customer Engagement

Originality generates **excitement and interest** among customers. When you offer something unique, it naturally draws attention and encourages interaction. Original ideas and services spark curiosity, start conversations, and create buzz—all of which lead to stronger customer relationships and brand loyalty.

5. Long-Term Sustainability

Being original fosters **continuous innovation and adaptability**, which are crucial for long-term success. Remaining agile by consistently improving your offerings and staying ahead of trends helps your business thrive, even as the world changes around you.

6. Intellectual Property Protection

Developing original ideas can lead to valuable **intellectual property** like patents, trademarks, and copyrights. These assets give you legal protection and a competitive edge, preventing others from copying your work. Intellectual property also creates barriers to entry and enhances your brand's value.

7. Emotional Connection

Originality creates **emotional bonds** with your customers. When your product or service is meaningful and authentic, it resonates deeply and leaves a lasting impression. That emotional connection builds **loyalty, repeat business**, and word-of-mouth referrals.

That said, while it's important to stay true to yourself and your brand, **always maintain respect and sensitivity** toward others. We're still here to **collaborate, uplift, and serve our communities**. Don't lose that connection with your customer base.

In my experience, **retaining a good customer costs much less than finding a new one**. If you expect loyalty from people, we as business owners must show that same loyalty in return.

Strive to be **known for something**. Create your niche—and work to become the **best in your field, subject, or endeavor**. This is what will set you apart from everyone else and keep you on the path to long-term progress.

Chapter 12: Learning to see Opportunities in Every Problem

In April 2018, the first Opportunity Zones were designated. They were created as part of the **Tax Cuts and Jobs Act of 2017**, which gave investors in lower-income areas valuable **tax advantages**. The real purpose of this program was to unlock capital that might otherwise be held back due to investors' reluctance to incur capital gains taxes.

Over **8,000 Opportunity Zones** exist across the 50 states and five U.S. territories. This is relevant because several of my upcoming projects fall within these designated areas. In fact, my newest shopping center, **Montague Plaza**, was partially built by leveraging this program. The Opportunity Zone designation helped **incentivize investors** to support my vision for a $4.3 million project in a historically underserved area of Raleigh, North Carolina.

When we develop projects that serve **minority and economically disadvantaged populations**, it's crucial to use every tool available to make the **economics of the project viable**. Many market-rate developers won't even consider building in neighborhoods like these. But I grew up in these communities. I understand the added layers of complexity that come with **urban development in distressed areas**.

Now that I've talked about what Opportunity Zones are, here's a **cheat sheet** on the **top benefits of building businesses within them**:

1. Tax Incentives

Opportunity Zones offer **major tax advantages** to investors and business owners. These include the **deferral, reduction**, and even potential **elimination of capital gains taxes** on investments made in designated zones. By reinvesting capital gains into qualified Opportunity Zone businesses, investors can potentially increase their **after-tax returns**—a big win for the bottom line.

2. Access to Capital

Opportunity Zones attract a **diverse range of investors** who are seeking tax benefits. This can result in **greater access to capital** for businesses operating in these areas—more than in other non-designated locations. The **influx of funding** helps support business growth, innovation, and long-term sustainability, particularly in neighborhoods that have historically been **neglected**—yes, even *in the hood*!

3. Community Development

Building businesses in Opportunity Zones doesn't just help investors—it helps entire **communities**. These projects create **jobs**, offer **essential goods and services**, and stimulate **local economic activity**. Businesses can play a **transformative role** in neighborhood revitalization, boosting property values, improving infrastructure, and enhancing **quality of life**.

4. Strategic Location

Opportunity Zones are often located in areas with **high potential for growth**. In Raleigh, for example, many of these zones sit along **major transit corridors**, often near historically Black neighborhoods. Establishing a business in such a zone can improve **access to customers**, **supply chain logistics**, and **market visibility**.

5. Workforce Development
Businesses in Opportunity Zones can forge partnerships with **local educational institutions**, especially **HBCUs** like **Shaw University** and **Saint Augustine's University** in Raleigh. With additional nearby institutions like **North Carolina Central**, **N.C. State**, **UNC-Chapel Hill**, **Duke**, and technical schools like **Wake Tech** and **Durham Tech**, the potential for **collaborative workforce training** is huge. Investing in **training and skills development** helps businesses meet their labor needs while empowering local residents with **higher-paying jobs**.

6. Social Impact
Opportunity Zone development creates a chance for **meaningful social impact**. By addressing **unmet needs**, increasing **economic inclusion**, and supporting **community programs**, businesses can actively contribute to **social equity**. In our case, this focus has improved our **brand reputation**, and I'm confident it can do the same for others.

7. Long-Term Growth Potential
Opportunity Zones offer **significant long-term potential**. As these areas undergo revitalization, demand for products and services tends to increase, creating new **expansion opportunities** and stronger **business viability**. Getting in early allows businesses to **capitalize on growth** and generate **sustainable returns**. But always consult **financial**

and legal professionals as part of your due diligence—these projects must be done right.

For years, I invested in areas with **no real incentives**. Before this legislation, there was no such thing as Opportunity Zones—so you can imagine my **delight** when this program became available. Because of my **experience** and understanding of what this means, I was able to take full advantage—and help others do the same.

Unfortunately, **many others don't know how** to cut through the fog of complex information to see how this tool can help them **and their communities**. Some people see a **rundown building** or an **empty lot** and see a nuisance. But I've learned to see the **opportunity** inside every difficulty.

Chapter 13: No, Such Thing as a Free Lunch

In my local community, we are surrounded by either **get-rich-quick scams** or intense, **feel-good remedies** for depression and pain. On almost every corner near the hood, you'll see **liquor stores**, **lotto stands**, **SKILL games**, **fish tables**, **CBD/vape spots**, **smoke shops**, and more.

Take a short drive into the **residential hood areas**, and you'll find men standing on corners selling an assortment of pain relievers and **illegal pharmaceuticals** to folks without prescriptions. Nearby, you're almost guaranteed to be approached by a woman—hooked on those same drugs—offering sexual favors just to get another hit.

This is **not a new problem**, and it's certainly **not unique to my city**. It's a **nationwide issue**, and in some places, it's even worse. The reason I'm bringing this up is to highlight the dangerous **promise of instant wealth or fast feel-good fixes**, which has ruined **millions of lives** and continues to wreak havoc on countless more every single day.

And this problem isn't **just in the hood**. In today's world, **no area is immune** to scams, substance abuse, or crime.

We must fight against **any false narrative** that tells people they can get something valuable **without putting in the work**. Anything worth having is worth **working for**, and the true price must be **paid in full—up front**.

Too many people fall victim to the **constant barrage of media images** glamorizing joyful people drinking, doing drugs, or engaging in violence—selling the illusion that these things are the answer to life's problems. In reality, these choices only **create new problems**—ones that cost you your **health, freedom, peace of mind, and opportunity**—and in too many cases, your life itself.

Chapter 14: The Power of the Tongue: Speak Life or Speak Defeat

The secret to success has been right under your nose the whole time. Every day, we hear friends, family, and even strangers say some of the most **negative and self-defeating things**— often about themselves. These comments are usually said jokingly or in a lighthearted way. For example: *"I'm so stupid,"* or *"I'm such an idiot."* What most people don't realize is that the **subconscious mind doesn't know the difference between a joke and a declaration.**

Every time you speak these words—whether seriously or jokingly—you are **speaking them into existence**.

If you tell yourself that you **can** do something, you're right. If you tell yourself that you **can't**, you're also right.

In the book of Luke, chapter 6, verse 45, it says:

"Out of the abundance of the heart, the mouth speaks."

This means that whatever is in your heart—when spoken aloud with emotion—**becomes your reality**.

We each have a choice to make: **Will we speak life, or will we speak defeat?**

It makes no sense to say one thing and mean another because unless your words are backed by strong, sincere emotion, they won't carry enough power to impress the mind and attract results. But when words are spoken with **conviction**, they become **creative forces**.

The most powerful tool we have for success is **literally under our nose**—our **mouth**. And the most important part of the mouth? The **tongue**.

As it says in Proverbs:

"The tongue is a small part of the body, but it holds the power of life and death."

That's not just a saying. That's spiritual and practical truth.

We must be cautious about how we use our words—especially when talking about ourselves or speaking negatively about others. Every word is released on a powerful frequency that vibrates and aligns with similar energy—immediately working to attract the reality you've spoken.

So speak **life**. Speak **positivity**. Speak **growth**, **love**, **power**, and **favor**!

When you speak, internalize that emotion. Let it become real energy. Couple that energy with words of power and **visualize the result you want**—then put in the work.

Because, as it's written in the Bible:

"Faith without works is dead!"

Chapter 15: Begin with the End in Mind

It is common in this day and time for most people to live day by day—just drifting.
No real plan. Just vague ideas with no concrete action steps.

This is a very dangerous and potentially costly mistake.
All success is obtained **step by step**. It's important to remember that **constant focus** on a desired goal is necessary.

The **mind is the most powerful tool known to man**. It has the power to create, if given proper guidance—or to destroy, when it gives in to negative energy.

For the sake of this book, we will focus only on the **positive, uplifting, and inspirational side**—which, when visualized and held in the mind with clear intention, will manifest into blessings:
Wealth, life, great health, abundance, and peace.

The image you desire must be **visualized in such detail** that the brain is almost tricked into thinking the experience is real—and has already happened—even before it manifests in your physical reality.

Every detail should be imagined.

Let's say your desire is to obtain a fancy sports car.
It's not enough to *just want it*.
Ask yourself:

- What does it look like?

- What's the exact exterior color?

- What does it smell like?

- Can you smell the leather interior in your visualization?

- How does the steering wheel feel under your fingertips?

- What does the engine sound like as it revs?

This visualization must feel **as real as possible in your mind**.

By doing this, you're developing your **power of constructive mental creation**.
You are literally creating your future.

The crazy part is—many people think this is a bunch of malarkey or impossible to do.
But the truth is, people are **already doing this in reverse**. They imagine negative things, and therefore attract negativity into their lives every single day.

Fear, doubt, and worry are magnets for the negative.

It is impossible to attract positive outcomes while focusing and giving energy to negative thoughts, ideas, or suggestions.

Each of us attracts the substance of our lives—so we may as well attract the **good and desirable life** that we truly want.

By beginning your journey **at the end**—with the desired result—you **pull what you want to accomplish into your present reality**.

The key is to **start at the end and work backward** from there. This process is called the **Reverse Engineering Pathway**:

You are working **from the future to the present**.

Chapter 16: Turning L's Into Lessons and Level-Ups

The secret weapon to building strong character and increasing your chances of becoming successful in real estate is learning how to **stay focused on the mission—even while taking L's**.

What are the L's? It's common to substitute the word *loss* for the letter "L." In business, examples of these losses include **levies, liens, lawsuits, and low credit scores**.

If you can stay courageous while going through these things, **you will develop an unshakable character**. I speak these words from experience. I've lived this reality and, unfortunately, been through each of these over my 30+ years in business.

Just remember: **don't panic when challenges arise**. Take time to process and assess the situation, then determine the best course of action with a cool head. When faced with big problems, we often panic and make decisions out of fear. Later—sometimes immediately, sometimes years down the road—we reflect on those rushed decisions and **wish we had handled things differently**.

Even though these things happen, we can't change the past. So there's no need to stay down about what's already done. That's like trying to live in the past. Instead, **chart a new course, learn from the experience, and move forward**.

Nobody in their right mind enjoys taking losses. But if you're going to build anything worth having, it's part of the process. Nothing teaches a lesson better than **a painful loss**.

When I first started in business, an older and wiser man warned me that, eventually, I would be tested by hard times and experience many ups and downs. In my ignorance, I told him that would never happen to me—I was too smart for that. I honestly thought he hated on me and was trying to wish me failure. That wasn't the case at all. He was trying to give me a heads-up so I wouldn't be shocked when hard times came.

Within five years, I was facing the roughest time of my life. I was taking L's in big ways. Thankfully, I remembered his advice. Years later, I told him about the challenges I was facing and that I needed some guidance. Thankfully, he didn't say, *"I told you so."* He had empathy. He connected me with the right people who helped pull me out of the fire.

I can't spend too much time talking about pain and loss because the purpose of this writing is to be **truthful and positive—and to help you win**.

So, here are a few **ways to turn a bad break around**:

1. Evaluate and Pivot

Conduct a comprehensive analysis of the areas that are affecting your bottom line. Look at market trends, your competition, customer feedback, and internal operations.

2. Identify Adjustments

Pinpoint specific areas where changes can be made to overcome challenges. This could include refining your product or service, exploring new target markets, or repositioning your brand.

3. Develop a Strategic Plan

Create a clear plan for implementing changes, setting measurable goals and realistic timelines to track your progress.

4. Communicate Your Pivot Clearly

Share the new direction with your team, customers, and investors so that everyone is aligned and on board.

5. Enhance Customer Relationships

Everything we do is for the customer. Use CRM (Customer Relationship Management) tools to gather insights into customer preferences, behavior, and pain points.

Keep them engaged through personalized emails, social media outreach, and exclusive offers. Ask for feedback through surveys or direct interaction—and respond meaningfully. Reward loyalty with discounts, promos, or early access.

6. Focus on Cash Flow

Review your cash flow statement thoroughly to find risks and areas for improvement.

Forecast your cash inflows and outflows so you can manage liquidity before issues arise. Negotiate better terms with vendors or seek discounts for early payments. Consider lines of credit, peer-to-peer lending, or factoring to stay afloat in tight times.

Back in 2008 during the recession, I had to cut discretionary spending and renegotiate contracts to keep things moving.

7. Innovate and Differentiate

Invest in R&D to identify emerging trends, adopt new tech, and improve the customer experience. Streamline your operations where possible.

8. Seek Mentorship and Expert Advice

This one is critical. Surround yourself with **people who will tell you the truth—not just what you want to hear**. Some of the best advice I've received came from older men in the business who gave me raw, unfiltered truth. I didn't always like it—but I always needed it.

You don't need "yes-men" when you're on the path to progress. You need a sounding board with wisdom, experience, and courage to give honest feedback that helps you grow.

Chapter 17: You Don't Hear Me, Though!

Ecclesiastes 9:16 states, *"Wisdom is better than strength, but a poor man's wisdom is despised, and his words are not heard."*

What that says to me is that in this society, unless you are successful—or at least *look* successful—most people won't pay much attention to what you say. Your words of advice and guidance will often be ignored, even if you are truly knowledgeable and a subject matter expert.

Regardless of what people claim, they usually follow the leadership and words of someone who *appears* prosperous. Appearance plays such a major role that sometimes, you can be judged by how you carry yourself—before you've said a single word.

Several times a day, when I'm driving one of my luxury toys, I get stopped by people asking what kind of work I do. I normally stop to answer, especially when it's a young person—hungry to succeed—who wants to make a change and a difference in their community.

But be very cautious with this habit of judging people by outward appearance. In every community, there are scam artists who, by all outside appearances, seem successful but are only using the image as a front to lure in and deceive future victims. These scammers often promise unrealistic returns in exchange for small or large investments—only to disappear and leave people broke.

There's an old saying: *If it sounds too good to be true, it probably is.*

Before you invest in any new venture, **do your due diligence**. Ask questions. If someone wants your money and they're serious, they'll usually be happy to answer legitimate questions without issue. If intellectual property is involved, it's completely normal to sign an NDA (non-disclosure agreement). In fact, an NDA is there to **protect the interests of the person sharing the idea** and should be considered a non-negotiable part of doing smart business.

The sad truth is that many Black historical figures never got the credit—or compensation—they deserved for the inventions and innovations that changed the world. Their concepts and ideas are still in use today, but their names have been largely forgotten. Many of these brilliant brothers and sisters died penniless, even though their inventions sparked entire industries.

Take, for example:

- **Benjamin Banneker**, a Black inventor, mathematician, and astronomer born in 1731, who created the first wooden clock in the United States.

- **Benjamin Bradley**, born into slavery in the mid-19th century in Maryland, who built the steam locomotive engine and taught himself engineering. Because he was enslaved, he wasn't allowed to patent his invention. Though he later received patents after the law changed, the world had already taken much from him.

- **Richard Spikes**, the brilliant mind behind the car self-starter. Without his invention, we'd still be hand-cranking our cars to get them going.

Let's not forget the sisters:

- **Mary Van Brittan Brown**, born in 1922, who **designed and patented the home security system**—a closed-circuit television setup that let residents monitor visitors and remotely lock doors. Her invention laid the foundation for today's multi-billion-dollar home security industry. Yet during her life, she received very little recognition and no real compensation.

These are just a few examples of how the **talent and brainpower of Black people** have been undervalued, stolen, or ignored. If justice had been served, **every heir of these pioneers would be a billionaire—or at the very least, a multi-millionaire**.

And the tragedy is this: There are *thousands more* untold stories of Black inventors in this country who never received a dime for their creations.

Today, armed with information and access to intellectual property protection, we must do everything in our power to **get credit and compensation for our innovations**. Not just for ourselves, but for our children, and our children's children. As the Bible says, *"A good man (or woman) leaves an inheritance to his children's children."*

In this age of advanced technology, **our youth should not be starting from the bottom**. They should have access to tools, resources, encouragement, and support to help them rise higher than the generation before them. That's the true meaning of progress.

Can you hear me now?

About the Author

James "Monte" Montague Jr. is a real estate developer, entrepreneur, and community builder from Raleigh, North Carolina. As founder of F7 International Development, Monte has spent over 25 years revitalizing communities and creating legacy-driven housing solutions. His powerful journey from cutting hair in the Southgate projects for fifty cents to building multimillion-dollar developments inspires others to lead with faith, build with purpose, and hustle with integrity.

Business Contact:

F7 Development, Inc.

📍 Raleigh, NC

🌐 www.f7development.com

📧 info@f7development.com